# Random
# Thoughts

*Other Books by Karen Royer*

Royers' Round Top Cafe . . . A Relational Odyssey

# Random

# Thoughts

Second Printing

ISBN: 1-57502-959-6

Printed in the USA by

3212 East Highway 30 • Kearney, NE 68847 • 1-800-650-7888

# Dedication

This book is dedicated to those who realize
they don't have a life but want one.
Getting a life is a life process.

# Acknowledgments

To Bud, my biggest cheerleader. He always encourages me to travel to uncharted territory. His support is unending. He's my soul mate. To Tara who believes in me. To Micah and Ashley who understand me. To Todd who listens to me, and to J. B. who laughs with me. To E. B., my muse, who writes with me. Thanks for all your support through ideas and thanks to our heavenly Father who lights the way. Karen.

Thank you Frank. You're selflessness is unending, your support strong, and your character noble. Thank you Brooke. You're so honest and inspiring. Thank you Austin. Your cereal consumption is as amazing as your sensitivity. My eyes see God through all of you. You contribute to who I am every day and encourage me to become what I might not have been. I love you. Tami.

Thank you Johnnie. Who read, drove, fed, cajoled, encouraged, and inspired us in countless ways. You're a real soul sister! Karen and Tami.

# Missions Possible Statement

In our fast-paced world where we are expected to perform to higher and higher standards, we have forgotten about the childlike qualities that got us where we are today. When was the last time you took a nap on a mat? Drank milk out of a carton? Painted with your fingers? What happened? You grew up and forgot how important play is to your creative process . . . and to your overall well-being. You got a job, started a family, paid the mortgage, and counted the days until life would be easier and simpler. But it hasn't and you feel stuck. The good news is that you don't have to wait until you retire or until your proverbial "ship" comes in. What guarantees do you have that either one of those possibilities will become reality? Play now, play hard, and go out with a bang. This book is a serious attempt to help you tap into your play reservoir, discover yourself, become more childlike, and therefore, more open to the possibilities of life.

# How To Use This Book

First, simply read the quote and think about your first response. This helps you focus on what you have believed in the past. Secondly, allow yourself to open up to the quieter, more intuitive "you". At this point, you may want to stop for the day and incubate on this thought. Later on, come back and read our thoughts on the quote. It's o.k. to disagree with us! But, this is a challenge to help you think. Then, if this thought "speaks" to you, do the exercise and somehow incorporate this into your lifestyle for at least a day. Finally, we've selected a book which explores or complements the thought at a much deeper level.

You may also use this book as dinner table conversation by reading the quote and asking for discussion. Explore everyone else's possibilities to your favorite thoughts. This is not for adults only -- get kids involved, too.

As you read through this book, some quotes or exercises may pique your interest more than others. We encourage you to linger as long as you need on those because you probably need to. Journal your thoughts. Underline -- write in the margins. Grow!

# The Visual Process

Random thoughts is written just like that -- one thought at a time. No order. No instructions. No right way. No wrong way. There are even symbols to help you digest.

These are our thoughts about the quote.
Agree, disagree, just think.

An exercise that you can do or not do.
We encourage you to try and incorporate it into your life for at least a day.

Recommended reading.
These are books that speak to the quote and, hopefully, they'll speak to you, too.

# Words

*Ambiguous.* Webster defines ambiguous as "having two or more meanings". It is when the rules are unclear and the answers are not black or white.

*Creative Energy.* Mihaly Crikszentmihalyi calls this "flow". It is when information comes into your awareness that matches your goals. This energy flows effortlessly.

*Creativity.* We like to think of creativity as being similar to the process of childbirth. It is bringing something into being. We like to focus on the process, not the product. It is a lifestyle.

*Inner Critic.* Your negative self who criticizes your projects and endeavors.

*Play Reservoir.* This is a place inside of you that some have called your "inner child". It's where you keep all your toys. As an adult, this toybox may be locked or you may have lost your toys. Finding that reservoir is key.

*Mediocrity.* This is simply another way of saying "average". It borders on apathy and definitely lacks passion.

*Mindset.* This is comprised of your belief system. Over time, it is difficult to challenge that way of thinking. Changing your mind has been called "breaking mental mindset".

*Synchronicity.* This refers to events that happen in life that are seeming coincidences. The emphasis is on seeming -- this implies that these events are meant to happen when they happen.

*Tap.* Connect with your creativity.

*There is more to life than increasing its speed.*
Gandhi.

Our culture doesn't reward the things that are really important. Our culture rewards high performance, social status, money, achievement, physical attraction, grades, and materialism! Don't buy into it. What's really important is what you're doing with your friends, how you're giving back, reaching outside of yourself, and achieving personal goals.

Take out your calendar or planner and a set of festive highlighters. Develop a color code for spirituality, family, work, and play. Highlight all your activities according to your new code. At the end of the month you'll be amazed how you're spending your time.

*The Zen of Seeing: Seeing Drawing As Meditation.*
Frederick Franck.

*Yesterday's meal doesn't satisfy today's hunger.* Unknown.

If you achieved all your goals today, what would you do tomorrow? That's what we do with retirement, isn't it? Most of us would like to retire healthy at 55 to a place with picture postcard qualities, but have insurance and enough money to fly across the world on a whim. But what's going to happen once you get there? You've changed. The town you're living in is not so bad. After all, you've spent a lifetime building relationships there and you can't sell your home because it has too many memories. You spent precious time you'll never get back planning for a dream that has lost it's luster. We change unconsciously every day. Sit down occasionally and realize it's o.k. to dream new dreams.

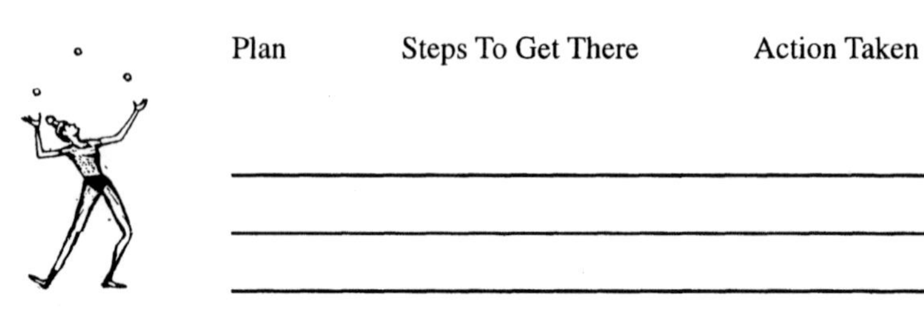

Plan    Steps To Get There    Action Taken

*Life Doesn't Frighten Me.* Maya Angelou.

*Know thyself.* Jean-Paul Sartre.

How well do you know yourself? Knowing who you are is foundational to tapping into your creative energy. So many of us settle for less without thinking about what we really want. Some of us have issues of unworthiness that keep us from pursuing our deepest dreams. It is difficult to be creative when you are stuck in a job you hate because it robs you of your energy. Some of us run from relationships because of abandonment issues. Perhaps you have issues from your past that you know you need to address. Those unresolved issues are an impenetrable wall that block the way to your true desires and wishes. Don't be afraid to seek help so that you can be all you were created to be. After all, there's only one wonderful you.

Write down your best traits, your favorite thing about you. Go on -- do it! Try to list 26 positive attributes -- one for each letter of the alphabet.

*Inside Out.* Larry Crabb.

*When you decide, the rest will follow.*
Unknown.

We make decisions every day. Are they small steps to happiness and bliss or just part of life? Decisions are powerful tools. Their usefulness depends on what you're building. You can decide to help build a Habitat for Humanity House, see New York City at Christmas time, exercise more, plant an all white flower garden, write a book, invest more in relationships, move to Canada, wallpaper the bathroom, clean off your desk, get organized, learn to fly, or simply go to the grocery store. WHATEVER you decide to do, just take the scenic route.

What's the first small step to making your decision a reality? Write it down. Do it!

*Making Choices*. Alexandra Stoddard.

*You may delay, but time will not.*
Benjamin Franklin.

Reinvent your life. How crazy is that? Quit your job, sell your house, move to Colorado. Are you dreaming? Dream on! Maybe you don't crave a radical life change, but you're starting to feel the life clock ticking. Don't wait any longer. This life ends too soon and it would be a tragedy not to begin it.

Change Your Life . . . Be generous, decide, play the lottery, try Feng Shui, change jobs, enroll in a class, take the first step, try liposuction, alternative medicine, cinematherapy, be still or speed up.

Think of two or three things you would like to change about your life, big or small, and write them down. Pick one and do it!

*Tuesdays With Morrie.* Mitch Albom.

*If it's not fun, don't do it.* Doug Hall.

Why not add some fun to your daily routine? Get some crayons and draw pictures. Feel free to color outside the lines! Try drawing left handed. Put a sponge on your desk to remind you to soak up all the great ideas you can that day. Pull out your children's toys. Wear a funky hat, funny tie, or wacky earrings. Read some joke books. Play a game of hopscotch at lunch. Find an old-fashioned top and take it for a spin. Draw with chalk on your driveway. Get a yo-yo and brush up on some old tricks. Paint hearts and flowers or write inspiring words on your bathroom mirror.

Try three of the above!

*Jump Start Your Brain.* Doug Hall.

*Life is not a dress rehearsal.* Alexandra Stoddard.

How many times have you heard your grandmother say "Where did the time go?" Most saved and planned for a secure retirement but many missed life along the way. How sad. Each day can literally be a new adventure. You're your own travel agent. Spend some Saturdays taking road trips instead of cleaning the house or mowing the yard. There will always be things that need to be done. If you have to work in the evening, read those reports while sitting on the porch swing listening to *The Village People*. Choose to be different, add color, and enjoy life. Eat *Lucky Charms* instead of *Grape Nuts*.

Take a spontaneous road trip without a map. Get in the car and go. Let your heart lead you. Stop along the way and discover.

*Around The World In 80 Days.* Jules Verne.

*Only when you say the truth can the truth set you free.* Marianne Williamson.

Why are we so afraid to speak the truth? Most of us have had an experience with a bad car salesperson at some point in our lives. The whole negotiating experience is like being boiled in oil and why must the salesperson keep going to talk to his sales manager anyway? Why can't we just deal with him? It's sort of like talking to the Wizard. Or, are you one of those who doesn't answer the phone because you fear a salesperson will call and you know you can't say no. Don't allow them to win by controlling your life.

The next time someone says to you, "How are you doing?", tell them the truth -- the whole truth.

Watch *The Wizard of Oz.* Afterall, you always had it.

*Love is not a feeling -- it's a verb.*Unknown.

Why is this so hard to believe? Why wouldn't you want someone to speak nothing but truth, be secure enough to put you first, and value the importance of the little things? If you don't expect a lot, you won't get a lot. It's as simple as that. Take relationships slowly. Watch for stop lights that say, "I'm not relationship material." If they don't act right before the commitment, they're sure not going to act right later. Like a friend said, "Just because you sleep in the garage, that doesn't make you a car." And, afterall, people say they love trees but they cut them down.

Write down all the people you know that have gone through a divorce. Don't you think it's time to value ourselves more?

*Men Are From Mars, Women Are From Venus.* John Gray.

*I will pick up the hook,*
*You will see something new,*
*Two things. And I call them*
*Thing One and Thing Two*
*These Things will not bite you.*
*They want to have fun.*
*Then, out of the box*
*Came Thing Two and Thing One.* Dr. Seuss

Dr. Seuss . . . what a wonderful free and creative thinker he was! If you need a refresher course on his imaginiative mind, pull one of your Dr. Seuss books off the shelf for a quick brush-up. People always say they want to think "out of the box" but what does that really mean? Thinking out of the box is radical thinking -- new and different ways of looking at the same old problem.

Read a Dr. Seuss book -- or two.
Go ahead, it's easy to do
Pick up a stack of Seuss
Go make yourself some juice
You'll be lighter when your through
Because you've learned to kick off your shoe.

Picture your life and the box it is in. What do the walls look like? What do they feel like? Then picture your life and remove the walls and barriers. Now, what do you see? Where can you go? Dream.

*Green Eggs and Ham.* Dr. Seuss

*The more we exist outside the system, the more creative we become.* Karen Royer.

Have you become "institutionalized"? Are your habits entrenched in ruts so deep that it would take a pole vault to scale the heights? We must work hard to counter part of a system of rules and regulations. It's difficult to tap into your creative reservoir when your workplace doesn't encourage such behavior. But you can keep your creative spirit alive by learning to inject a big dose of humor into your workday.

Try putting two things that are totally unrelated on your desk, like a bowl of Christmas balls in July and an old rusty wrench. They'll inspire conversations. Your coworkers will start talking but more importantly you will get your brain going in directions that inspire new thoughts and new ways of looking at things. Try it tomorrow.

*Pour Your Heart Into It.* Howard Shultz.

*Everyone needs a playbox.* Karen Royer and Tami Hons.

Playboxes can be customized, individualized, and even fantasized. They are filled with all sorts of things -- things to help you change your mindset and maybe even transform time for a few minutes. You can use them to shake up your coworkers at another dull, stale meeting where everyone is tossing around the same old ideas or you can use them to embarrass your family at the most inopportune time. You can definitely help others get out of their box by pulling out your box.

Create your playbox. You can add *Play-Doh*, squoosh balls, finger paints, glow in the dark stars for your ceiling, stickers, *Whoopi* cushions, marbles, a *Slinky*, scented markers, bubbles, water guns, jacks, jump ropes, and even your favorite rocks or seashells.

*Living Juicy.* Sark.

*You can discover more about a person in an hour of play than in a year of conversation.* Plato.

The chains we create keep us from enjoying the fullness of life. Why not take a cooking class, start wearing hats, volunteer at a hospice, hospital, or school? Why not plan a trip to Europe, have a teddy bear picnic, take a course in something you know nothing about? Why not fill your bedroom with candles or twinkle lights?

Try one of the above -- or something you've never tried before.

Read something you wouldn't normally read.

*When people show you who they are, believe them.* Maya Angelou.

Did you ever stop to think if all people would just do the right thing, what kind of world this would be? People show themselves to us everyday, but for various reasons we don't believe them. They're under pressure, they didn't really mean it, or surely they didn't know what they were doing. We forget that leopards don't loose their spots. Maybe if we started seeing people for who they are, realizing their strengths and weaknesses, and understanding we're not all built alike, we might enjoy some of the paradoxical surprises life has to offer.

Identify the most difficult person in your life. Change perspectives by finding just one positive trait about him or her. Focus on that trait this week.

*Bold Love.* Dan Allender.

*Creativity is piercing the mundane to find the marvelous.* Bill Moyers.

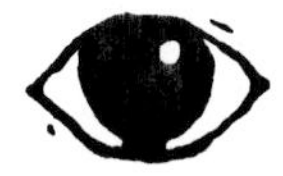

Researchers tell us that ninety percent of five year-olds test as highly creative. By age seven, this level drops to an astonishing ten percent. Past age eight, only two percent of kids exhibit a high level of creativity. Early creativity can be shut down by schooling. Messages like "color inside the lines" and "there's no such thing as an imaginary friend" teach kids to conform early in life. But all the blame for a short supply of creativity cannot be given to schooling -- home life has a significant effect on creativity as does the myths surrounding creativity.

Was there a particular teacher who encouraged you? If you can find him or her, write them a thank-you note.

*Growing Up Creative.* Theresa Amabile.

*True humility is esteeming others as higher than yourself.* Paraphrased by Johnnie Gulig.

People are sometimes filled with fear, jealousy, and bigotry because they need to feel more important than somebody else to feel good about themselves. That's so hurtful. Truthfully, we are here to create small miracles for other people every day. You may not be recognized for this kind of heart-full attitude but you will know -- just know -- in your heart that you are encouraging others by speaking genuine words of care, concern, and happiness.

Compliment someone today. You'll be amazed by how it make's you feel.

*I Corinthians, Chapter 13.*

*The most profound thing in a person is the will that person has.* Oswald Chambers.

We are surrounded by silent heroes. The co-worker that has dutifully come to work every day for the last 20 years probably won't be a contender for a Nobel Prize, but he has run the race of patient endurance. He's been satisfied with his job in a *Federal Express* kind of world because he invested his time, talents, and energy into his family and friends. Know who you are. Look for the faithful, be inspired by their perseverance, and be a light to others.

When someone attacks who you are, don't buy into it! Know what is true about yourself and believe it!

*Make The Connection.* Oprah Winfrey and Mark Green.

*True friendship is seen through the heart not through the eyes.* Unknown.

True friends inspire you to become what you want to be. They move heaven and earth to be there for you because friendship doesn't mean casual acquaitance -- it means a lifetime bond. After all, as Antoine de Saint-Exupery said, "It is only with the heart that one can see rightly; what is essential is invisible to the eye."

Remember a time when you've seen with your heart. Did you carry it to fruition or did you reason it away?

*The Little Prince.* Antoine de Saint-Exupery.

*There is no They, just us.* ex. Graffiti.

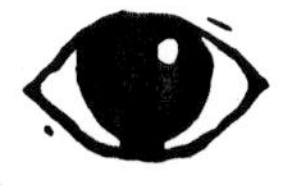

We live in a society that's all about blame. It's about bad childhoods, sexual abuse, mental anguish, and bad television. It's time to rise up and own our problems and mistakes. We all have them and that's what makes up "us".

Get up every day. Do your best. Help others. Go to bed. Stop trying to find a bigger purpose than what you've been given. Stop blaming others for your problems. Celebrate your life.

*Oh The Places You Will Go.* Dr. Seuss.

*Life's what happens while you're busy making plans.* John Lennon.

We lose so many wonderful moments while looking for the perfect ride. Magically, if we look through different eyes, we see things with amazement and gratitude -- a walk down the driveway to pick up the morning paper, your child's first band concert, a moment when something you said made a difference, an unexpected letter, a surprise gift, movies, or great quotes. Slow down and refuse to contribute another second to this hurried world. Set a pace for others to follow. Life is precious.

Try keeping a journal of special memories you want to savor - ones you don't want to loose. Create a book of special meal times, complete with menu, pictures, music, table settings, conversation, and the most important ingredient -- the guests.

*Royers' Round Top Cafe . . . A Relational Odyssey.* The Royer Family.

*Everyone has a dream but life has a way of making us forget what they are.* ex. Wild America.

We all wanted to be cowboys, princesses, kung-fu fighters, actresses, and pilots when we were young. Did someone break into our world and steal our dreams and fantasies away or did we simply misplace them? Give yourself permission to dream about what you really want whether big (like a trip to Europe) or small (dinner at McDonalds) but allow yourself to dream those dreams. Dreaming is essential to your overall mental well-being.

Write yourself a "permission to dream" slip -- like a prescription for allowing dreams. Fill in the blanks with your dreams and wishes.

*Living Your Life Out Loud.* Sally Rasberry.

*All I have seen makes me trust the Creator for what I have not seen.* Ralph Waldo Emerson.

Have you ever marvelled at the universe or wondered how many perfect coincidences had to transpire before you met your life partner, moved next door to your best friend, or even discovered your favorite food? This world is a huge place and it's made up of billions of people -- each trying to make their own way. Dreams and visions can be met the same way unlikely relationships transpire, one coincidence after another.

Think of the last time you encountered a coincidence -- now, don't think of it as a coincidence, reframe your thinking to allow synchronicity.

*Synchronicity: The Inner Path of Leadership.* Joseph Jaworski.

*Don't let others affect your purpose.*
Pierre Moranza.

It's easy to become obligated and over-committed. Carpools, meetings, errands, homework, committees, and parties can be engulfing. But are they part of your purpose or your destiny?

Separate yourself from at least three things that you're currently doing that don't affect your purpose.

*Releasing Your Potential.* Myles Munroe.

*Life is a big canvas, throw all the paint you can on it!* Danny Kaye.

Who is your favorite artist? Have you considered how you are painting your own life's canvas? Do you see yourself creating a modern painting in the style of Marc Chagall or Pablo Picasso? Or do you "paint" in abstract symbols like Joan Miro or Wassily Kandinsky? Does your lifescape have the depths and mystery of the Grand Masters? Whatever style you prefer, think about how you would like your masterpiece to look -- is it framed -- how?

Find a medium in which you would like to work -- oils, watercolors, fingerpaints, or *Play-Doh.* Play with your creation. Let it represent your life up to this point.

Go to your local bookstore and thumb through one of your favorite artists' work. Get inspired.

*Be a good listener. Your ears will never get you in trouble.* Frank Tyger.

How are your listening skills? When someone is relating a story to you, do you listen intently, focusing on what he or she is saying -- watching hand and eye movements while responding with positive cues such as head nodding and grunts to encourage the person along? Or, instead of listening, are you thinking about what you are going to say to "top" the story? Our listening skills need to be exercised to keep in top shape just like our muscles. If we really listened to each other, we would probably drastically reduce the need for therapists. Studies show that many clients say of their therapists, "He's the only person who ever listened to me." How tragic!

Practice listening to someone today. Focus on that person and their story, not your response. Listen, really listen.

Read the remarkable story of a remarkable lady, *I Shock Myself!* Beatrice Wood.

*The harder you fall, the higher you bounce.*
Unknown.

In *The Lion King*, Rafikki said to Simba, "The way I see it, you can either run from it or learn from it." He had a valid point. Our culture is so afraid of failure that we will do almost anything to keep from failing. The truth is that failure, properly managed, is a great wellspring of creativity. It's been said, fail often in order to succeed sooner. Learn to regard failures as stepping stones to success. This mindset will help you set the fear of failure aside.

Think back to a time in your life when you thought you failed miserably. Think of all the emotion you felt at that time. Now, with the perspective of time having softened the experience, write down what you learned from that time.

*The Maverick Mindset.* Doug Hall.

*Dream as if you will live forever. Live as if you die today.* James Dean.

You have just returned from the doctor's office with startling news. You have only one month to live! You rush around in a panic thinking of all the things you haven't done or things you've left unsaid. You plot out the next 30 days in order to correct this myopic view. You call friends and make amends, you write love letters to your children and family. You take a spontanous trip to Machu Picchu with your best friend. In the midst of great sorrow you are happy with the choices you are making. Two weeks into the month, you receive a phone call from the doctor's office. They made a mistake -- you are just fine and forever changed because during that short time you learned how to truly live.

What would you do if you had only 30 days to live? Write it all down. Do it!

*I Heard The Owl Call My Name.* Margaret Craven

*Life is like a box of chocolates. You never know what you're going to get.* ex. Forest Gump.

Have you ever wondered why the world fell in love with the fictional character in the movie, *Forest Gump*? He wasn't an intelligent man but he was an honest one. He was made fun of, yet he chose to think the best of people. Choosing to see good instead of evil is a conscious decision. Forest had the childlike courage to make the choices we always hope we will make but usually don't for various reasons. Just imagine if we lived by *Gumpisms*.

Be a *Gump* -- just for a day and carry one of those old suitcases if you have one. Tell the truth all day long.

*Forest Gump*. Winston Groom, Rebecca Todd.

*What a strange world this would be if we all had the same sense of humor.* Bern Williams.

We're becoming clones. Designers dictate what we should wear, directors decide what entertains us, and a good advertising firm could encourage us to buy absolutely anything. Where's our originality? Why do we want to be just like everyone else? We're not born the same. We're supposed to be unique creations with our own sense of self. Instead, we're spending lifetimes trying to be people we're not.

Be a trendsetter. Buy something to wear that YOU like, not something everyone else is wearing, and wear it to work.

Watch *Saturday Night Fever*. If John Travolta can wear that white suit -- so can you!

*If you obey all the rules, you miss all the fun.*
Katherine Hepburn.

In Karen's creativity seminars, she often asks participants to make an egg stand on its end. This always produces a flurry of questions that begin with, "Is it ok to . . ." The purpose of the exercise is to show that we impose rules upon ourselves even when no one else does! When someone gives you a project and the rules are ambiguous, allow yourself the freedom that you have been given to explore the project for all it's worth. Allow all your silly ideas and then hone them down to what you think is needed. We often put ourselves in the box when no one else has -- climb out of it!

Make an egg stand on its end without censoring yourself. You can't use anything to prop it up. It needs to be freestanding on its end. Go!

*A Whack on the Side of the Head.* Roger van Oech.

*The universe is made up of stories, not atoms.* Muriel Rukeyser.

Have you ever thought about the stories that comprise your life? Have you encouraged others to think about their own unique story? If you like a good novel, then you like a good story. What is yours? Stories have great power to help someone hold the mirror up and see his reflection without being preachy. Stories move us to a relationship with someone else. When a therapist - friend was questioned about his work, he said, "Really, it's not that hard. I just tell stories until they begin to see themselves in the story. When one can empathize, then one can move from being the victim to being in control of one's destiny." If you don't tell your own story, chances are that no one else will. And, after all, there is only one unique you.

Think of how stories play a part in your life. Then, comprise at least one story that you think will interest someone else. Refine it. Go tell it!

Read a story (biography) about someone you find intriguing. If that's too much freedom, read *Goddess: Martha Graham's Dancers Remember* by Rob Tracy.

*On any day, at any moment, you can change. That is the power of grace.* Oprah Winfrey.

People can change. Most don't because they underestimate their abilities to make change happen. Others let their past interfere with their future. Casey Treat said, "Your windshield is a lot bigger than your rearview mirror." Wonder why? Let's face it, past is past and we can't change it -- but we can wallow in it. Although wallowing might feel good for awhile, eventually we may begin living there and if that happens, we can't contribute to society. How can the world become better without us?

Name something about yourself you don't like. It could be where you're living, your comb-over hair-do, or where you take your cleaning. Write it down. Now that you've named the change -- do it!

*What's So Amazing About Grace.* Philip Yancey.

*One of the secrets of a happy life is continuous small treats.* Iris Murdoch.

We love treats! You need to care enough for yourself to treat yourself often. We find that when we do this, we are able to give to those around us more effectively than when we don't. What's a small treat? It depends on your budget so it can be really small -- like a new set of scented markers or a bar of your favorite soap from your favorite bath and body shop. Or, if your budget allows, treat yourself to a pedicure or a new bottle of cologne. Once a year, splurge on a big treat for yourself and a friend or yourself and your spouse -- like a trip to the Big Apple to see the latest Broadway play. It's more fun if you make your big splurge a big surprise. Treats depend on where you are. If you have no money, treat yourself to a sunset viewed from the highest point near your home or go to the park and watch children play. Treats come in all shapes and sizes. Treats don't depend on money, they depend on your imagination!

What are five free treats you can give yourself? What about five small treats under $5.00? Write them down and do them. The big treats are easy to think of. It's the small ones that require some thought but the rewards are huge.

*Simple Abundance.* Sarah Ban Breathnach.

*For sleep, riches and health to be truly enjoyed, they must be interrupted.*
Jean Paul Richter.

There is nothing quite as wonderful as a good night's sleep after a bout of insomnia. There is refreshment from being forlorn when things look like they just might work out. Or, when the richness of a relationship lost is regained through an odd twist of circumstances. Perhaps you made a doctor's appointment because you found an ominous lump only to find that you need to restrict your caffeine intake! Having experienced all of this, we know the joy that comes when you still have something that you thought was lost. The trick, we believe, is to appreciate these small blessings of life before they are interrupted. Learn to cherish what you have instead of pining for what you don't.

List three simple things that you take for granted, like air, rainy days, and kind gestures.

*She's Come Undone.* Wally Lamb.

*Respect is something you command, not demand.* Phil McGraw.

Do you want a new job, another title, or a degree? Why? Sometimes we go out of our way to gain respect. Job titles don't earn you respect, doing a good job earns you respect. Degrees don't earn you respect, what you do with your degree earns you respect. Esteeming others instead of esteeming yourself earns respect. Doing the right thing instead of turning a blind eye earns respect. What's the moral of this story? Don't do half a job. Attack everything ahead of you with passion.

Take a few cleansing breaths and think about the last thing you did that you REALLY felt good about. What was it?

*Don't Worry, Make Money.* Richard Carlson.

*To do nothing is the most difficult thing in the world.* Oscar Wilde.

Creativity experts tell us that one trait above all others is necessary for creative output. It's tolerance of ambiguity and it means that you stay in a problem long enough for the solution to present itself. Usually these are relational problems over which we really have no control at all. We don't own the problem. What may be difficult for some people to tolerate can be easy for another -- so don't compare! The next time you are faced with a problem see if it might resolve itself with a little tolerance of ambiguity.

When faced with the stress of a difficult problem you must endure -- go get a massage!

*Creating an Imaginative Life.* Michael Jones.

*For all man's pretentions, his very existence depends on six inches of topsoil and the fact that it rains.* The Cocklebur.

You could die today. There could be a tornado, a car crash, or a quirky accident, and life as you know it could be over. We emphasize so many things about our lives, but what it all really comes down to is dirt. "Man thou art dust and to dust thou shalt return."

Push up some dirt (soil to the professionals) and plant something. Anything.

*It's Always Something.* Gilda Radner.

*Remember, if you don't plan your own funeral, someone else will!* Karen Royer.

Have you thought about how you would like to be remembered after you die? Chances are, you haven't, but you should. It's going to happen and who better than you to plan your own funeral! Perhaps you would like everyone to wear purple rather than black. Or perhaps you want your best friend to read your eulogy. Maybe you would like to write something for the program. Possibly a great storyteller is called for or a marching band playing "When the Saints Go Marching In". The point is, if you don't plan it, someone else will. Think about it.

Write -- or at least begin to write -- your own funeral or memorial service while you still can.

*How We Die.* Sherwin B. Nuland.

*There's nothing quite as wonderful as a succinct epitath!* Karen Royer.

Karen spends time wandering through old cemeteries, looking for stories and for great epitaphs. She has stumbled onto some wonderful ones, too. Some favorites are "I told you I was sick," "She lived a life of ambiguity, I think," "This-that but what's important was the dash." She wants hers personally to say "She lived her life out loud" or "She was an artist of being alive." Tami's isn't quite as deep, but then again she doesn't usually frequent the cemetery, either. She'd like hers to say "She always tried to do the right thing." Our husbands think ours should both say "They spent too much money."

This should be no surprise! Write your epitaph.

*The Book of Eulogies.* Phyllis Theroux.

*Hope deferred makes the heart sick.*
Proverbs 13:12

Hope keeps your dreams alive. Dreams are essential to one's well-being but there is a balance between keeping your dreams before you and changing those dreams as circumstances and conditions are altered. What kills your hope? Perhaps you sabotage yourself because you really don't believe you deserve anything more. Maybe you think the risk is just too big to take so you never attempt to reach your dream. Possibly you just don't know where to start.

Dream on! What is one dream you would like to accomplish and would -- if you knew you absolutely could not fail? Keep the dream alive by listing the steps to get there. Begin.

Go rent *Mindwalk.* It will blow your mind!

*Myths have tremendous power to shape our lives.* Rollo May.

There are ten top myths surrounding creativity -- myths that shape our lives. For instance, perhaps you have told yourself that you don't have time to be creative or that you weren't born with creativity. Or maybe you've thought that creative people just arrange flowers, they're weird, or creativity is gender biased. These creative killers and others keep you from tapping into your innovative side. Refuse to believe them anymore!

List myths surrounding your creativity. Wad the paper up and throw it away! Don't make these myths a part of your belief system anymore.

*How to Catch Lightening in a Bottle.* George Gamez. If you're feeling particularly intellectual, read *The Cry for Myth* by Rollo May.

# Creativity Killers

"We have always done it this way."

"Yea, we tried that once before."

"It will cost too much."

"We just don't have enough time to implement it."

"It won't work."

"It will take too much effort."

"Management won't like it."

"It's never been done before."

"You can't teach an old dog new tricks."

"Get back to reality."

"I see your point but . . ."

"Let's come back to that idea later."

"You are always dreaming."

"You will never get that idea off the ground."

"Good idea but it's not practical."

"That's not your problem."

*Our chronic busyness keeps us from our dreams.* Don Hudson.

Our society is driven to distraction as we move from errand to errand, meeting to meeting, and workday to workday. When we get home from work, we flip on the radio or TV because we are not comfortable with the silence. Our culture lives at what is called the "delta" brain wave level. Translated, that means LOTS OF NOISE! To be able to tap into our creative side, we need to approximate the "alpha state" which occurs when you are dropping off to sleep or just waking up. Your great ideas await you here! You can teach yourself to reach this state but it requires quiet. What are you waiting for?

Spend five hours (ten would be even better) without electronic noise (no television, CD players, radio, phones, pagers,etc.). Sit. Be. See what happens. Or, if you are really adventurous, go spend a weekend on a structured silent retreat. Check with your local monasteries for information. They can help you find one in your area.

*The Cloister Walk.* Kathleen Norris.

*Those who never get carried away should be.* Malcolm Forbes.

Do you ever get carried away by something you love or are you afraid of how you will look to others? Perhaps you are afraid to be passionate about something. As adults we are afraid to tap into that spirit of playfulness because we are afraid of how we will look. Get rid of that inner critic and play! Make mud pies, go fishing, hug a tree, dance the jig. We don't forget how to play because we grow old -- we grow old because we forget how to play. Begin a rebellion. Fight that urge that makes you grow old.

Go rent your favorite animated *Disney* cartoon. Watch it.

*Passion!* Roz Van Meter and Pat Pearson.

*I don't want to get to the end of my life and realize that I just lived the length of it. I want to have lived the width of it as well.* Diane Ackermann.

Seconds turn into minutes, minutes turn into hours, hours turn into days, days turn into weeks, weeks turn into years, where does time go? Most people live life as if it were a dress rehearsal for something else. This is it! Resist the temptation to settle. Know that every night when you fall into bed that you have lived the width of that day. Know that you have squeezed every drop out of that day that was physically, mentally, and spiritually possible. You will sleep better!

Are you living the length of your life? List some areas you would like to be wider in your life (except your hips!). We're not talking superficial; we're talking about soul searching.

*Daring to be Yourself.* Alexandra Stoddard.

*Mediocrity is self-inflicted. Genius is self-bestowed.* Walter Russell.

Mediocrity is easy. Excellence just takes a little more effort. Albert Einstein said that great spirits have always encountered violent opposition from mediocre minds. And why wouldn't they? If everyone just settles for the ordinary, then everyone becomes mediocre. Fortunately, those great spirits usually have the guts to endure the opposition from mediocrity. It takes great courage to stand alone with your beliefs. It takes great courage to think alone. It takes great passion to translate those dreams into reality especially when the crowd is safe; the crowd is easy. The crowd will kill your individuality.

Commit yourself to excellence by refusing to be mediocre. Think of an area where you have allowed mediocrity to win. Commit to change beginning now.

*Defying the Crowd: Cultivating Creativity In a Culture of Conformity.* Robert J. Sternberg or *Living Above the Level of Mediocrity* by Charles Swindoll.

*The wonderful thing about the game of life is that winning and losing are only temporary -- unless you quit.* Fred Mills.

Persistence is one key to reaching goals. Many successful people will tell you that the only reason they succeeded in an endeavor was because they simply refused to give up. Thomas Edison "failed" at his goal of making a light bulb almost 1500 times before he succeeded. When asked about his seeming failure, Edison replied, "I haven't failed. I have just learned 1499 things that don't work." Albert Einstein said that the only difference between him and someone else is a sense of curiosity. He said that he never stopped asking "why?" And, then there is the great story of Winston Churchill who was asked to give a commencement address. The person giving Churchill's introduction spent too much time, in Churchill's estimation, talking about all of Churchill's accomplishments. When Churchill finally got to the podium, he may have given the greatest speech of all time when he said as he pounded on the podium, "Never give up! Never, never, never give up!" And, then he sat down.

Become a why-ner! *Why* not learn a new language? *Why* not learn belly dancing? The next time you want to try something new -- do!

*Unstoppable: 45 Powerful Stories of Perseverance and Triumph fom People Just Like You.* Cynthia Kersey.

*Often people attempt to live their lives backwards: they try to have more things, or more money, in order to do more of what they want so that they will be happier. The way it actually works is the reverse. You must first be who you really are, then do what you need to do, in order to have what you want.* Margaret Young.

Do you feel stuck on the "I need more" treadmill, thinking that more equals happiness? Your neighbor got a brand new sports car. Your best friend just spent three months touring Europe. You? You just got to buy milk after touring the grocery store. Someone has said that being genuinely happy about someone else's good fortune is the most difficult thing to do. We become jealous and while we may utter our congratulations to them, inside we wish we could have what they have -- then we would be happy. Things don't make you happy. Only you can make you happy. Be who you really are and do what you know you need to do.

Are you happy? What do you think will make you happy? If your list involves acquiring things, reframe your perspective to being instead of buying. Be rich in friends; invite some over!

*How to Want What You Have.* Timothy Miller.

*Never fear shadows. They simply mean there's a light shining somewhere nearby.* Ruth E. Renkle.

Aren't you glad that most of the things that you fear never actually come true? So if the rate of probability is so low, why spend negative energy worrying? Sometimes when you ask someone how they are doing, they will reply, "I'm doing fairly well, under the circumstances." Well, get out from under those circumstances! Realize that dark clouds pass through your life but that the blue sky is always there. There are many times that we simply don't get a reply when we ask "Why?" or "Why me?" Understand that these times will pass. You may never know why. You may, however, choose to be under the circumstances or on top of them!

Make a list of your Top Ten Worries. How many of them are beyond your control? Make a commitment to park those things over which you have no control in a "no load" zone.

*My Utmost for His Highest.* Oswald Chambers.

*Nuture your mind with great thoughts.*
Benjamin Disraeli.

Aristotle said that we are what we repeatedly do. What do you repeatedly do? Do you nurture your mind with a continual diet of television or do you spend time reading things that will improve your life? Throughout this book we have given you great reading ideas to nuture your mind but we have only scratched the surface of what is available. We haven't even mentioned the classics. Resolve to spend a year reading a classic a month. Or pick a favorite author and dive in deep. Try a steady diet of C. S. Lewis or George MacDonald for a year. We promise this will have a profound effect on your daily life if you will make the commitment.

Pick a classic and give it a try.

*The Brothers Karamazov.* Fedor Dostoevsky or *Les Miserables* by Victor Hugo.

*The truly free man is he who can decline a dinner invitation without giving an excuse.* Jules Renard.

Can you say no to something you don't want to do? Or are you a "yes" person who says yes to everything and is continually frustrated because you can't do it all? This frustration takes its toll, not only on you, but on those around you. Overcommitment leads to overcomplication in your life. Learn to say, "I'm sorry but I can't." No excuses, no reasons, no explanations. Identify your priorities and say "no" to everything else.

Say no to things you don't want to do. Try it for at least a week.

*The Artist's Way.* Julia Cameron.

*It's kind of fun to do the impossible.*
Walt Disney.

We wrote this book. That's unbelievable considering the worlds we live in. Can you imagine how people looked at us when we told them we were writing a book? They looked at us with even more disbelief when we invited them to go with us to Chicago when we become part of *Oprah's Book Club*. We dreamed big and found it necessary to speak those dreams. The more we professed it, the more it became reality. When you hide your dreams sometimes you forget where you put them. Of course, we're still waiting on the *Book Club* deal, but the ride has been great!

Grab your high school yearbook. Remember who you were. What dreams did you have then?

*Einstein's Dreams.* Alan Lightman

*We must learn to live together as brothers or perish together as fools.* Martin Luther King, Jr.

Discrimination is still going on. Maybe for some us it's just too big a job to tackle but unless we start trying to make a difference, we'll be no better than previous generations. When you were a child, did you want to use just one color? Probably not. In fact, you probably fought with classmates over colors. Maybe our Creator felt the same way; his picture would be much better in many colors. And, afterall, he invented creativity.

Find a coloring book. Try coloring the entire picture in just one color. What do you see?

*Creating From The Spirit.* Dan Wakefield.

*You are never given a wish or a dream without also being given the power to make it come true.* Jules Renard.

We believe dreams and visions are messages sent from your heart to your head. Some of you think they are just your body's way of escaping reality while you sleep. Maybe so, but maybe not. How often has someone tried to explain something to you and you muted out the sound of their voice? How often have you seen a child cover their ears and chant, "I can't hear you"? Maybe we should all listen to our hearts a little more closely.

Get up each morning and for at least a week write down what you dreamed the night before. No dreams are o.k. Do you see a message or a pattern emerging?

*The Artist's Way.* Julia Cameron.

*Act as if it were impossible to fail.* Dorthea Brande.

Someone has said that there is nothing as dangerous as an idea -- when you have only one. Learn to look for the second right answer. Many times we will use the first idea we think of because it is easy. Learn to stay with a problem -- push the deadline to the very end. Ask for input from others -- seriously consider it. Trust that the solution will present itself if you are actively searching for it. If you don't have a great solution -- learn to wait (Go out on a limb. It's where the fruit is.).

Write down a problem that is begging for a solution. Write down seven or eight possible solutions. Put the list away for awhile and think about it. Come back to it several days later. Which solution appeals to you now? Map out a strategy to get there.

*101 Creative Problem Solving Techniques.* James M. Higgins.

*Our creativity is not a cute thing for weekend dabblers in the arts; it lies at the essence of who we are. We are all creators, and therefore we all have good work awaiting us.* Matthew Fox.

There are countless ways to increase your creativity. Karen talks about her four favorite strategies in her creativity seminars. Capturing - Learn when your creative times are and capture your ideas when they occur. Keeping notebooks handy means you will be able to jot those great ideas down as they occur. Challenging - Learn to challenge yourself by putting yourself in situations where you are likely to fail to some extent. Cultivating - Encouraging your creativity with a wide variety of learning repertoires. Step outside your comfort zone to new experiences. Capsulation - Surround yourself with things that you love; things that stimulate your thinking process; books, poems, pictures.

What is your most creative time of day? When do your great ideas occur? Think about it. Buy notebooks and fun pens to put in a conspicuous place to capture your ideas.

*The Grace of Great Things.* Robert Grudin.

*A painting is never finished -- it simply stops in interesting places.* Paul Gardner.

Perhaps the above saying is indicative of a book, too. It's difficult to know when and where to stop but we feel that this is a good time! There is a Chinese proverb which says, "I hear and I forget. I see and I remember. I do and I understand." We hope that by doing the exercises and reading the suggested books, the ideas will take shape in your life in a way that is uniquely you. We hope that you have enjoyed the product as much as we enjoyed the process.

For more books
OR
custom created
Seminars
on
creativity & problem-
solving.

Contact

Karen and Tami
at
409·764·0604

email: dreamer@phoenix.net